Or Scissel

First published in the United Kingdom in 2018 by
Shearsman Books
50 Westons Hill Drive
Emersons Green
BRISTOL
BS16 7DF

Shearsman Books Ltd Registered Office
30–31 St. James Place, Mangotsfield, Bristol BS16 9JB
(this address not for correspondence)

www.shearsman.com

ISBN 978-1-84861-621-9

Or Scissel

J.H. Prynne

Dost Dialogue with thy shadow?

Timon of Athens

Shearsman Books

ALL SUCH TO LIFE

All such to life consuming
    as all were true
in air passing and lifted
    besprent with dew

Nor lavish nor in unison
    even at the shore
for giving its world over
    for this and more

By leaf turning, its colour
    so clear to find
in itself its fond allure
    to love assigned

Such voices set fiery
    within, and through
the field of folk unwary
    in shape as true

CLOSE SHORN

Close shorn, give enough granulate
    ever to calm or assemble
unstricken, by company resting,
    arms folded for so as can

Who would in readiness turning
    to maintain the line
of breath out to then clarify
    in jacket new yet worn

Suit yourself they say as plentiful
    uninterrupted, aspired win
powder reception they freely do
    so frequently now be seen

All forward then uppermostly
    hold out, to save other tame
detachment, from main body temper
    in season coming to term

SWEET VERNAL

Went to mow a meadow, extended grasses
      in scrap cut down, swiftly
down and down. Bent to lie, scented
      cry hay vocal for quick in a box
as if so never let go.

Take good incremental surplus up
      steady parallel concise, fixed
to expect completion not childish
      count, went, sweet vernal far
and freely even for far away.

For see the moon remounted in favour,
      bright in its day-box, yet to play
just one silicon bonding dilatancy
      pack and fold, here to single out
any good reason, first off to be.

BEYOND DOUBT

Lace over to search the part ready-made
by sentiment ever for and so for
to easement in despite, to call
in provocation hearing the short cry
all to make ready all beyond doubt
mix and restore, severally utter
even though newly wishful retain.

See further, see link alignment
repairing to measure the cost
of finding truly when to recognise
how swiftly & gainful it could be done:
patch to discretion, refinement
individually next already in sealant

attach across reflected morning light.
No anthem mostly discovers this
single type, aver openly set down
to bring back, outlying custody
in colour revetment, remission
not well in purpose fortuitous; so
marked for display, never so fair,
by credit of melody in session taken.

All the way by glances, line and shout
without manufacture however soon
to rising brilliant departure, snap fast
a child's permission; don't yet care
for act to vanish, prefer both of them
immoderately. Persistent or now
ambulant attain the flow partition.

Glaucous rosette in mastery, in profile
as catch in the throat dividing
how to part up-front, assented trifle
pardon this chill. Whether of two inform
bone retraction catch advance, gather up
category spill ahead they will do it
to mitigate the doorstep plantation.

TO EYE APART

To eye apart fine arrow key you know leaf
greeted in fading search ahead, acres ready
set aside, nothing happens here. Eye-brow
lucid to miss low density, synthetic honey
spread remember within walled crannies: fork
up paint both hands, manner graft to pack
by willing sips, stand up, nocturnal at beat
first. As besides termly will either, neither.

PLATFORM

Straw promise to vowel, up then why or be
forward on bind,
                    advent kind rested fare so
         by for, in the by of
         leaving over, and must
               declare did telluric
         agree for the consort partner ahead,
stem will accept as raised to a latch
offended on its ground near equal. The level

says, how many chopped cell forms want
           profuse redolent capture, risk attach
               link to match in start at twin
         limbic falls, go to further lets be
attend, accept reflecting promote so, yes accept
               is soon wake or grant

along the present invited retroflex hang over
         sky turning to this, visible succession
           plays for cost permit
         in fever, open must mark eyes now
outermost earthen flaw give mine the rest.

FOR THE TRAVERSE

For the traverse then extended turning stairs
at body-search into resume, step out win folds
or brisk the path risen courtly; elbow slice
attaching for lit. Never pantiles yet foremost
to partnered their corolla both limits each bite
sheer will trample headed text, purchase what
relives inspection. Will fix its mantel. Braced
matter parting fair crest in favour, probable by
any much less provided. Or like holding a hand
outward palm centred overt taper, mission now
forbid them. Voice shaking to likeness stain
as for side planted above, by each other plying
almost figured checks, no little temper offence.

OTHERS WILL

Carmine slept underneath provision, or we too
not reluctant evenly displaced the whole intimate
fuse cancel syllable, to this depending ever yet
rigid. Arrive to take flame induced, at impasse
settle quickly surface bail in a novel temper fob
give it back full amount ours to say, first esteem
corundum tooth exchange. Bone easy acquaint
in a surgical detachment, all crowded forward
to liken blemish aquamarine at limit restore
for so for mischief, the whole time. Likely insert
finish now and next by effort splint to relative
fugal and wipe, clear and down. Gain seed-time
advancement generous option, share margin on
pulse unmatched or not yet, at least batty foreign
allow expulsion. Indeed should we next assign
what comes to finish nearby, so to merge, roofed
over tin foil guarantee in purpose of colour,
dredge in advance signal clip. Would do both gap
settlement to be seen overtly, aspect trim up
to stitch, up to snuff. Long awaited for good reason,
part for part cut finely cheer acceptance aspect
foremost even relative, to point best allocate, to
claim anyway. How is this known, to amount in
late perspective one for neither, rise up or try
arrival as others will, or do. Mercurial finish
all of them marking in place of refuge better late
than for vision earlier dent, traffic. Reflective
tremor in flashes, margin brilliance out to sea
flim-flam grateful well back nipping across
highlights. At ready fashion outwards familiar
pass to passion, motion interrupted whose turn
wants less for more, unless late fusion will.

EACH NEW RETORT

Apart estate limit hooding frame to go for
list over, their keel apt in cut manner why
elated preventive, further on. Resemble
the whole time, on a side provided, degree
assimilate master pleading, its known plane
loose to meet. Exactly brave out, not yet so
soon to call a long cost observance, inter-
lude set by marker unmissed, inaction. May
wait until each new retort best anecdote tell
their own dispersal cautionary, luminary
pitch to part market, did you. The over deep
farewell risk in semblance, all of rate visit
to be first periodic welcome, in rain yet
track of its horror benefit refused payment.
Cloud uplift stack in order trim and eager,
breath for hers and ours. Together ajoinment
relic partition, every next moment donated
in what they found for repair, their best
mixture. Keyboard start back in notice, again
like this, culminate incident parenthood.
They all grow in frame on a side generous
mimicry, all in good time.

DASHBOARD FLOWING

Rasp to pinnacle dashboard flowing, in glow
of like seclusion, this will prolong its near
measurement in top after its best array. To be
noticed bright flank refit assuming, glimmer
in cornea engrossed to tilt, its tendency be-
side its own vested motion, fast enough even
by matching settlement. All will run amounting
to its fit low parallel, chorus fleet approving
by time of rapt enclosure: forward before back
then both above each other, can so better, be
graded ahead. Be sure to trace a complementary
fuse path, as will sink to a ground uplift;
lean on this vantage, strike margin checks at
count for credit in passion submiss, give or
be given outwardly. By flow who would know
this at once, phosphor insertion gradual runs
to completion, yield ready otherwise to save
as opportune. From the heart valve dash down
so below at threshold search, convergently
by friendship, blow to vanity. Open ridges
to trace and face in needful acceptance, to
sing and run parlance presumed to each by
life idiom, quickly and early concession; eye
to assimilate radiance, in perfusion of known
brow terminal, all-over peak coverage affront.
Shelter while still in reach. Adjust by matched
data off to discover leverage evenly prefigured,
to set fully the crest by entrance markings.
It's to be known as would fold up before hand
signal, reduce dismay to minimum browbeaten
improvement, gauge what's now visible to field
in pointed focus evoked – all the runners admit
this consigned better finish, ahead of reward.

DARTING

Previous and virtual now absorbed into a self
at large as fluent across the bound there allowed,
in course of fed with tributary not optimal but so
retrieved. Beyond insistent convergent is can be
ready, darting withhold, delay for donative you will
cancel presumed listen, feature outward. To why
or not livid brow lapped to a reach, sit in circle
will be soon enough spoken of this, open passage
burnt in unclaimed flash demise. All to meet there
so in row to bereft passion enclosure, flow in sorrow
past headwater make a dent abruptly, go better by
cured bacon included now first. The others in lane
give not silently, the task in stolid recognition even
yet to resist a clamour grievance. Crowd beyond in
large at the gateway, instrument to break by waiting
in unitary harmonics probable no less. Forgiven been
abrasive nearly alleged of plural to breathe or ahead
from pressure, side to side approaching hold back
the treat foremost, to be known. Open the flap pre-
cautionary versed incision, to listen however will be
operant in mass acceptance, must both so for sure
quickly prepare by abandoned light cone. You know
inflamed with attraction justly in time, our time
only perhaps, on a ledge fastened. The reason desired
will be enough, rolled out did you say in want, well
dream yet so below, hardship visible. Look there,
see to know, to go truly previous and virtual, yes.

NOT FAR

In a cross light yet forward for latency
met front lit over surreptitious again torn,
their plenish counter primate, scramble
try to speed diminish, led to brilliance.
Why or not excepting the promise fortune, as
well keep denial affection, scripted marker
affirm, all can part. Leafy shadow slips
cheek insidious hardly what's to listen, if
balance restored. Evident compression does
completely make sufficient arch to brow,
trefoil shining low down by the foot print
purchase revenue, aromatic sonic precedent
amounts to and neat beside the same or as
not far off. Fibre root shiny packing, when
found in pasture light-crushed volatile
slice to allocate a strip pacing, advance
to first place once pattern tread. Likely
or end reach the back light shadow play,
in bended compensation absterge revoke
all of their relish: eye-bright see better
what goes on ahead.

WAIT TO ARRIVE

Another seldom profuse retracted entire, in total
reclaimed running on forward slightly undeterred
or at least to be made up to full crescent foil. You
know foremost led invention this and next advent
reach out aspect product we know by hollow marking
conjecture, likelihood. Crush abstemious contrary
for all mortalism ready in line to take, to make
aware if listen well, to the onrush. Immense toy
of fancy press-stud variant, give back rescript
or massive exchange dispute. She will, she shows
the whole payoff, run close to title deed tantrum,
agile delirious fortify pressure to ex-limit margin,
to arrive first and for stay over like elfin tracks
in brazen near reluctance; admonished in recovery.
Confer with shared instinct, outside in shade deeper,
mend the gate, new at its task. Decree for under dark
pursuit envisage as in tank stored first protection,
ever right, ever known, condensed. Give a chance ahead
to miss a beat, street dropped alert in knife plumage,
meet to skim fairly in true uppermost acumen.

LAST PRESSURE OUTCRY

Said both on arrival as negligence reversed, to uncover
this with branches fallen and strewn, how else make dif-
ferent paths for them, pacify the headland shelter. Will
this be enough alert, crested by permission unreached,
locked in with shares deemed in readiness, further even.
Can be grasped for right converging allergy, for back
tendence as remission was it, cold humour in the turn
of earth to grade and meet alternate. Never default
in heart new in place, old seen there, price out. Up-
ended did you before concession, to give where lost hardly,
nil final attach sub-loyal this time make early deliver
at incident descent all will give to ford of a stream,
will know and justify by review absolute. At any time
of purpose approaching closer, hold out promise elected
to float in cloud billows, so many at contrast for courage
in title to generate the similar rocking path sensible.
Or in page not finish, fish spool will reach welkin, margin
can only amount to both at the pair-threshold, with
threaded clamour this too will outreach itself, to close
the passage against its own default. Will gather motion
against break in force, estoppel to look back utter
the name lost onwards to refund, offensive payment held
in check before all arriving surrender, above all weapon
to see and weep, there. Never less, for the last pressure
outcry, room for company conflicted average for start,
shallow breathing foreknown in limit prevailed, infold,
angle. Diverging set to accept by tune variance, wanted.

NOR THAN

Nor than double, open suffix to overturn new
patent to go there, saving beside or left on,
accepted precious for unturned did you reach
at last to meet; none alone take limit take
mine to ground, recently make fail pitching
monotone remission, for finish crowd compose
your roof. Will believe attending trial base
trail alongside to ban the way and slide over
nor lost nor broken, off lesson at cost ever
lose in sunny rising, its ream statistic by
fast trill risen in premiss there. Likeness
through to cut a path, cover service telling
pale to prowl below; bordering to miss his
fanatic crawlers without trace pack recourse,
leaving in deflection later yes across both
maps stripped in count freely, mile upon mile.

HOW SMART WE ARE

As ever still how smart we are, to come, to linger
as slow as daylight lasts each for respite, known
and even unknown, light the way. Bounty in plenty
up to pass by the revenue silence or close, founded
within above, given fast by choice, dotted notation
come to this by a line referred. Ember in mind, ash
wind-blown under marked brow and brushed back, never
cancel if time allows foretelling, buoyant to search
profoundly under foot would it be, by now. Lay out
in care wish to single by solo integrated life-spell
all light of morning, know better, meeting the range
with sibling trachea uncorrupted. Along the pathway
the creatures guide us, intent to wind and find, by
this case after that, pattern flow in cloud equal
to watch, laminate over the path heretofore glided up
and foregone; blood foray occlusive indignant careened
for just employ and scare, for clip where in dismay
no faring as well, so to go, on.

QUEUE UP

Rife and solemn where they part, catching
in time by order, of level polity; wait
in turn, the rest will reach to grant
accord compelled by residue beside entail
forfeit dark planet, optimal in company.
What's left to reckon one by one the further
cranky branch, limit first indulge abstain
in warranty. Go by the same track-marks.
Brow in fetch amounts to discreet arrival,
watch divided manifold, infill. Brim over
reduction shortage holds steady circuitry,
not urgent but dutiful seen from the front.
First come entrancement, open door pursuit,
key-fast. Extra to gravity swung inward,
aside voices arrest by note provision have
been there in purpose fashion, suffix en-
hancement. Is that amusement to hit marking
on the axis or further still, in bid for
levity has been part for whole, rest for
remainder, now all found. Example given
and taken, allowance trod down to ground
additive mission was it, unless the target
defeats its own singular investment.
They queue up for a share, over to claim
by allocation, who would that be by civil
solid grasp infirm or not, no difference.
Matter to crumple at loss to cross its own
level or limit view, up to partner in go
first then later, turn about the headland,
there. Did or done at brow escapade, even
solemn antic prorogue its continuance,
wind and weather permitting. Grandiose
talk to make advancement, all risks set
to subdue their own natural offence.

CUT AND STITCH

Shake by word and both, for this or these right
before the avenue, in colour to match up and for
concession flame arising, flicker if random as
not seldom, the parameter all soluble never be
even in part at the riser. Restore mostly the
same reproof, ready in line for sweet scarlet
arm and leg, spoken like the first arrival yet
even to mend and concede, know why and so know
less, put in place. Don't consume too soon by
expected parentage, with to mask the children
wait as latent patience to bridge their chance
as before was set in line, this way up. Casual
moment steadfast to reach in for desire, into
the front lighter, the same colour. Suited by
its regular match, looking easily good and even
for what's to mark incident, in a standing off
back to reach so far as ever, as trim to quite
fit near enough. Selection measure forthwith
more calm now, to yield by free will pleasing
on the whole review, of discovery so to forbear
lighted up, shared out. Along the avenue first
the entire train pieces together yes willing
be there resemble crystal top-up attachment
to be next ready amendment enlarging fulsome
entangled cut and stitch, sample. Even so all
due lineage, enough by sill bonding, to let
or fit each way suture patch further, into
whether the same or close. Grasp yet to need,
need to observe, perfectly serious cryptic
even when fully wakeful, count the cost with
limit masking withheld.

YET WHY NOT

Never or, will to it, or nerve throw past most
over soon after, and grasp again offensive
likely before over mud downwards cut, snip
relative next to time beset play genuine it
break: out by remiss ever sever gastric flux
do for provide, gainful lax all never acute
assert at more elate better still. Instinct
by step cost not for before to press or grill
tell strike blood flatter runoff, lever assort
it piecemeal, assent to deduct mud in grind
both under anterior the step previous stop
ever to ever. To ever step will decline for
one to meek repair furtive, few than certain
angular saw, in drive term relation or so
frequent casual fit. All not chosen pit limit
disfigure, late fill near total better wait
party to quick, not early river custom,
tepid and flow. Insist did rim-perfect as
few ever will before not soon, holding wrist
in front, look back taken. Rapid converse to
apex get climate some to die even before pat
list, shunt up weather climax remittance
flex not yet, ready. Up to step never level
incline wanted, condign else in gene pair
be for return upper parkline, all in sudden
afford to run. Ever not even not so ready
tacit permit, later outflow emit the step
will break will over will, not or so yet it
in this permissible livelihood.

LARK ADVENT

Bar first and second therefore climb or tell
to over tame any and firm, late mine inform
for ready, near torn to hand, leave now upset
do serious soft starving, prefigure ulterior;
    Sweet to listen, use mesh caress both folded
tideway grant why, furnish stay this to ever
finish or famish until avid work file availed
in swathe impure, split up, vision abrogate;
    Of blame at black tops careen to fault, pine
by share taken muted duct, us so to entail
as shall we, but canted over in thin limit, to
return score access agree banish, quicklier;
    Racing to hand, un-laid late bite as braving
    Wild reject obtuse thrown down whenever on.

ZINC OPTION

And despite twin to gem in such placement,
along the sun-drift, at the turn nearby run
across it with a soft tremor galvanised even
high and brittle; splinter alteration all known
beyond range incessant as slower for removal,
perish in parallel, squared off. Indignant both
in stock over elevate without pause for dial
later before due moment, perfunctory if by
measuring zinc option, beyond the gem-tilt
ice crevasse. Not reluctant by match willing
as would all be or variable; button furnace
steel chasing, defect for prospect indexical
home on the range in company expected abate-
ment accession roaming sense acknowledge,
make pack and fasten. Refract fully possible
to get close, alternate dispossession to
the upper frank reach, brow in mark not yet
or notable, in quake hot furnace new-broken,
offended. Declare vertical certain pitch
want no more for hunger makes contortion on
every side, despite censure or because of
its absence, to pay entirely on the nail ahead,
open. Weld inlay dangerous to carry forward,
deal unfound until by surprise uncovered,
on the floor keep up: necessary parclose. How
otherwise deal fair or first before, go there
extenuate by staunch prior permission, your
feet dangling.

MAIN–STREAM

Necrotic valency, this time round the flaw
placed first, inculcate latent chances, suf-
fusion by issuance merit advance, simulate
aversion: has surmounted obstinacy before.
Delinquent fluid settle instilled, monitor
hardly grimace, top-most. Let be accepted
on charge, relative to holding maximum in
main-stream trivial parsimony grip tight,
warrant the distance defeated at a random
walk, room for elbow in judgement arrested;
prompt for search primal retention, path
to border the stream bed, never scruple
to drain the wound's slight closure with
incentive add to leave; incremental record
foretold and ascertained by dressing, care
for sentience dig out a trench and shutter
it you'll see fast. In promise observe
closely, do what's true esteem all down
by provident attachment, fitting accom-
plished display. Treasure by treatment,
value-added resistant matching variation.
You do know what you find by revolving
trial, as waiting time rescinds the marks
that show deterrence, all the way. How you
know is not known, but so is so and ever
will remain.

IN A PLAN

Over to put a single aperture, by its even
mark to be given, to attach all will clearly
be set and taken in good time. Afford another
you might, all the whole arrangement but for
either to go allegedly, probably around however
cannot ignore or depute, because that's turned
in a plan so warm, already. Stream and climb
as tap ah so gently, to a finger rise advancing
part to entrance, come to faster charm you know
sibilant fixture, fore-brain, assign safe brim.
Patchwork amends the colour chart you'd not
pause at this, be generous no finnick tappet
make to amount just rightly consonant would be
in line for arrival, for effort. Future in plant
up to the limit intone in permission fast to
say and say ready back tremulous, all over in-
cidental by guarantee please to be, session
unbounded to the doorway; push forward upper
slope both ways gather it indigent compression
cool to brow head-wave, back. Yet accepting
visible perforate adjust will all hear close to
a full assembly, stay at this reversal given out
enough to join up near to may and may, time
out of reach, to come in. At child care will all
in touch, over be not converged, ambulant
take it on perfect offer; neighbour division.

THROAT NOTATION

Fortunate orphic resentment gathers dust,
hesitant river get in line, coy singing buzz
larynx fault diffraction, close measurement.
You heard the same sounds, underneath attend
vanquish or stipple in a choice prepared, sur-
charge furious deep down heavy in waiting, in
footprint tracement, incision. Did you care
to find out how many if they were equivalent
in recess darkened clue member, resounding
to her cuff just our poor luck: each in watch
for the other, at cave mouth donate pining
sink to the mark pinchbeck illusion, incise
shade plummet descending by nectar guides;
throat notation late fabular discontent. Of
incessant here or thereafter tuning up so
to play so to hear, voiceover entreated for
her own sweet sake or due still approximate
tribute fire-play. All fuel counting up on
the river be open in streamy flow, wet stones
and the woman calling, for now our plaintiff
ask debate, returning echo fixative. Wind in
flow and know besides incline perpetual first
come first served by estimate subdued fission
and teeming, frankly to a careless fault, never
going back. Look up, you'll see beyond un-
certainly, inform loss adjusted.

ENTITLEMENT

First ticket was known to him, holding up
in stub to match remedy, conduce entitlement
cast aside. Reprieve day by day pitching in,
curt lucid odium, before parody lays its mark.
Grip fast, journey to justify all spent out,
blood fusion segregate primal shortage, dabble
in wrath. Others will soon see what's missed,
without care, focussed ahead as soon as scan
returns. Bract detain addendum, try out a kick-
start vital pitch affray, dress antic wounds.
Crisis pushed down to nothing, foreseen parted
efflux incriminated far ahead, violent before
called to account. Throw out the whole folio
of greedy shots, his total abandoned chances
in tariff marking, pulse specific blockade
to beat back wasteful casualty. Reject the
promise exchange pedigree, thick saline in-
difference, however advanced.

KEEP ALIVE

Evident in repulse and concentric why
delay loop, fair bay shining, distorted
catchment each of them loose meander to
beckon foreign and line-up. Partnership
makes amends or excuses, how otherwise
colourant restores pensive agreement to
invoke unhurt recension by divisional
separate tenancy. They perturb the others
by sharp echoes, in scarf boastful drive
while fast fading presumed to announce
a patois assignment: accent-free. Alike
why in access reverberated, plentiful
earnest task fetched as per novel request,
notion to vision cohort fluorescence hers
to keep alive. Cloth squares yield their
rank order, give away a plain sequence
by meticulous activity; planning the steps
never too soon on a classic dorsal air
repayment. Part for whole, installation
holding sunlight in fetchwork inner decay
risen to it, first off, be in tune early
bird-song. Ruff up the trill as gleefully
augmented, will if she can in bel canto
attend blameless retrieval, outwardly calm.
Why would she not, by agreement fast in-
clined, not even scratched, rebate flung
off as omission breaks apart the shell
of fancy, quelled if needed.

OVERLAY SASH

New assure azure perform out of the corner
active intaglio memorial, get in line and stay
put missive affront malachite, flake. Yet lit
streak presumptive knee joint not so often
pedal the team confers to save space all indeed
sensibly capped. Ethiopic pearl sumptuous vital
leader flexed cloud base, flicker critic adds
animus they stand and watch, greedy if else
crude batch from leisure resected and unmute.
Better be terrified instant dressed out in fear
partition lapse, will cut you out of play de-
vice reclaim, anticipate destruction before
its level share. Be first or nothing, calorific
overlay sash by spent delivery, expensive did
you instigate fixture. Did you want it, banal
measure desired like the others cooked up, in
new fissure under forfeit, is that consumed
alongside store deprivation, would you even
notice italic if leafage obscured debenture.
Want this alone with otherhood visible purchase,
coercive appointment wrist burn, coverlet
pricked up in fashion trinket.

CHANT MEASURE

Tamper-proof evangelist all of them why-ever not
mean ingrate, replete too, restriction metro division
hardly in avoidance, foot-print in levity. Livid
furnace, all smoke shored up arising come right
out patiently ground to scraps, in the mincer, turn
in full view at front, at most. A wave of dilute
resemblance will grant a pause before cause to be
ahead by waiting fraction, late to satisfy; right.
They do all know even if late proclaimed, ever
tardy passage of salt, moist crust or blinking
furtive ingression. Tear out the line markers, if
replaced for aggregate one by one, neural ply, out
to get back. Finish with flourish, wave overly
let them or most ring out wild, back incipit
where not already resumed. You can slantwise
see that all of them hitherto will rip the cover,
anger plot grist to beauty in the face. Pray up
violent by chant measure, foolish rotation merely
established and greedy. Are they for even so
placid, other shunt aside and refracted sink
down harmful if yet diminish now and then,
excess confabulate, outright and limpid shower.

WE DO

Alight get set to fasten and impugn knit temper
astonish; we allow finally like all the others,
their retracted storm to cloud over. Did you see
that or catch turbulence whirled upward, cream
horizontal luft where we contrive best impression
going on through. There are vacant steps at inter-
val, follow trifle spick and span, crass. Amaze
too, aggrandise bright frequency in pack grimoire,
finger and thumb catch as catch can, soon out to
plan better spin stud enticement actual. Lattice
tremors eagerly forward, ink rising with tube
in hand, slow down tempest within conspected
grievance at the blame in cautious subtraction;
alliance exceptional draft annoyance run-time,
ray tilts. Upper partial extra striking all off
memory lit up silhouette flex protection first
downpour in name only, care to pick one quickly,
stricken forehead under brim recognisance where
so in note, turning out not to belong here should
late intern culminate; we do. As level pathway
both more tilted and near under-water, trodden
in fancy alliance, inveigle what you almost
will not give away, insinuate. We shall confirm
and lean aslant streaming the brook's demeanour,
casually while there's time, or fate single, or
yet later invited and ever intrinsic, ever full.

FOLLOW TURMOIL

Such fabric so torn, for tune by hazard chrome
in line feeling to part if not ready cavil time
watch, level shift cirrus reflected even when
soon whether practice longing to send, find, make
way by extreme aspersion. Better by next dis-
covered, open frame sedulous unlikely, cater for
other sentiment midst of life itself so early
waiting, waiting as will call to a sift-point
or now and then after, loyal. Brim at full regain,
follow turmoil or judgement, size enough capture
in scale. Take off the rest overnight vivid profile
disjunct and bright inflamed, it is known evenly
replaced, truly held. Could also be upper wrack
best in reach penitent by disclosed admission,
anticipate exact at birth. Darker trim first cut
away felt and tremble, many voices steeped there
in blue uprising, new cloud in its clue, search
entire forgiven unwilling but enough. By late proof
has birdlike review deployed, so flown to fledge
ambition, never too late within. Cordial bypass
rapture outwards in company select as verified,
presuming or yet by confirmation from parallel
inflicted, relented, sight self-made as brevet
ever find. Or this or that pretext set up in view
quickly, living colour first applied to like,
demonstrate, gather the threads once still bright
already and torn.

THE WAY, FORWARD

Levy accept countenance over this near
hill promised will the breach make up
for missing parts, forward to slope,
steep under guard. Did esteem design in
grateful addition loose the remedies
on top, not sufficient unless right in
capture fortitude. For drastic delete
askew, offspring few cloud fringes, less
moisture crepitate main wrong. Admit
returning balance to claim alight at the
stand illusion, at once or last revision,
don't resist too soon. When in reflection
mirror fold finds its due place in scale,
all in nurture, a plain tale on the mend.
Notice will all of them down-hill, scent
of rain creeps inward, over the sill
arrested or wary. Procession amounts and
grounds, whether disturbance reaches
high up in fixed delay, for cover and
over limit summit, raise the stakes in
what's to be seen yet clearly still enough.
Beyond play of fracture, profession lift
concealment water flow and grow by match
of a wanted seam, release as can be open
to latch or weir. In new place love what's
added on, paramount attach loyal acknow-
ledgement. If beyond doubt, hand-fast
care for rising profile again temper not
to excuse eye fortune or its near double,
chance occasion benign for steep native
pertinency rapid into transit endowed
subsistence. The way, forward step-fast,
hand by clue in hand.

www.ingramcontent.com/pod-product-compliance
Lightning Source LLC
Chambersburg PA
CBHW021946040426
42448CB00008B/1263